CLAIMING KIN

The Wesleyan Poetry Program: Volume 83

CLAIMING KIN

BY ELLEN BRYANT VOIGT

WESLEYAN UNIVERSITY PRESS
Middletown, Connecticut

The author thanks the Vermont Council on the Arts for an individual grant that al-
lowed her to complete this book.

Acknowledgement is gratefully made to The Gehenna Press, the publisher of a
limited edition of a broadside of *Tropics*, and to the following periodicals, in the pages
of which a number of other poems in this book were first published: *Arion's Dolphin*, *The
Colorado Quarterly*, *The Goddard Journal*, *The Iowa Review*, *The Massachusetts Review*, *The
Nation*, *Northeast*, *The Ohio Review*, *Rapport*, *The Sewanee Review*, *Shenandoah*, *The Southern
Poetry Review*, *The Southern Review*, *Twelve Poems*, and *The American Poetry Review*.

The publisher gratefully acknowledges the support of the publication of this book by
The Andrew W. Mellon Foundation.

Library of Congress Cataloging in Publication Data

Voigt, Ellen Bryant, 1943–
    Claiming kin.

    (The Wesleyan poetry program: v. 83)
    I. Title.
PS3572.O34C6   811'.5'4   76-5944
ISBN 0-8195-2083-7
ISBN 0-8195-1083-1 pbk.

All inquiries and permissions requests should be addressed to the Publisher, Wesleyan Univer-
sity Press, 110 Mt. Vernon Street, Middletown, Connecticut 06457.

Manufactured in the United States of America
First printing, 1976

92 91 90 89   7 6 5

For my family

CONTENTS

I

II

III

I

TROPICS

In the still morning when you move
toward me in sleep for love,
I dream of

an island where long-stemmed cranes,
serious weather vanes,
turn slowly on one

foot. There the dragonfly folds
his mica wings and rides
the tall reed

close as a handle. The hippo yawns,
nods to thick pythons,
slack and drowsy, who droop down

like untied sashes
from the trees. The brash
hyenas do not cackle

and run but lie with their paws
on their heads like dogs.
The lazy crow's caw

falls like a sigh. In the field
below, the fat moles build
their dull passage with an old

instinct that needs
no light or waking; its slow beat
turns the hand in sleep

as we turn toward each other
in the ripe air of summer,
before the change of weather,

before the heavy drop
of the apples.

AT THE EDGE OF WINTER

Vacant cornstalks rattle in the field;
the ditches are clogged with wet leaves.
Under the balding maple, toadstools
cluster like villages; their ruffled
undersides are brown. Inside,
we prepare for children: the clean
linens, the perfumed loins,
the aphrodisiac are ready. The cat,
our pagan daughter, has brought
her offering—the half-eaten, headless
carcass of a rabbit; its bright guts
bloom on the back porch step.

Rich November! Under the stiff
brown grass, the earth's maw
is full of tulip bulbs, hyacinth
and crocus to mull and ripen
these long months in deep freeze.
This is our season of opulence.
Festive, extravagant,
we'll spend your creamy seed
like the feathered milkweed blowing open.

Smeared with rabbit blood like a pagan,
I hack down the last new shoots
of the rosebush and arrange a bed
of rose and red cedar to scent
the fertile wound of the rabbit, lying
open and ready, primed for the winding
sheet of snow and the restless track
of the gray creative worm.

ANIMAL STUDY

The cat sleeps stretched out
like someone's fur piece or rolled up
warm as flannel. She can sleep outside
on a flat rock, full belly up, claws
pulled in, soft neck exposed.
She dreams of how she will slink
through tall grass without disturbing it
and discover there with her famous eyes
a rabbit for her pleasure or a mouse
whose rapid breathing gives it away.
Gently she will embrace it,
one arm around its shoulders,
the other moving gracefully to strike.
Or she thinks of the lovely birds, swooping
and gliding, and how she will leap up
higher and higher, over the clothesline,
her arms elastic and extending themselves forever.
And waking slowly is like coming home
to sit on a patterned rug and wash herself.
Exquisite, invulnerable—
like the spider spinning his shimmering filigree
or the clear mosaic of the snake's imperial head.

BLACK WIDOW

Heavy in her hammock, she makes
ready for mating. All black,
black love in the pit of her
eye, she lolls at the center,
a soft black flower.

Her lover rounds the corner,
he has directions, he knows
what he's after. Small & dapper,
he climbs the high wire.
His careful footwork strums
the chord of her lair.
Each step closer sends
her the message, she opens
for him like a cloud.

Done with her, he wakes
to her massive body & wants
out. But with his seed,
alas! he has lost his fleet
foot, his map to the maze.
The wires hum their report:
meat in the net. Her hulk
moves in black hunger
across the steel-ribbed snare.

THE HEART IS THE TARGET

for Louise

Hunger drove you across
the savannah and into the rainy
forest, sweating for prey.
As if this heat were an ally;
as if desire were a weapon.

Now you have reached the densest
vegetation. The path behind you
has closed like a curtain of water.
You have come upwind of your quarry.
The birds, with their passionate
language, announce your arrival.

Flushed by the chase, you lounge
on a viny cushion. Above the belly's
salt-lick, your breasts thrust forward
their wine-soaked centers. You strip
to the waist—a wash of light
against the green canvas. Soon,

in a murmur of branches, a figure
approaches. He sights the white field,
aims for the left breast's two
concentric circles. Then the pull
of the dark, centripetal eye.

DELILAH

It wasn't the money or their silly
political speeches. I planned it
long before they came to mince
and whimper into their spit-stained
beards. What would they know
of power? Such thin sticks for my
magnificent boar, swinging a jaw-bone,
smashing and driving—ah, Samson!
your loins' heat, the sweet weight
of your thighs. . . . That I could tame,
outwit, be stronger than *that*, I teased
the secret out. And in the early
morning, while the Philistines
leered from the fringed curtain,
while the royal harlots swayed
in their tents like frail-stemmed
flowers, while laborious wives molded
the meal-cake, their bellies warped
with children and children clutching
their slack breasts—in that hour
of last darkness, dressed in satin
split to an oiled thigh, I drove
my whetted shears to your sprawled
heap and the manly seat of power.

PREPARATION

The Bone-man lives in a stucco
house. He ticks his heels

on the cold terrazzo floor.
He parks his ragtruck

in the yard, instructs his crew
on the white telephone.

I am training my dog
to attack the red-capped hunter

bearing his long package.
I am training the tethered jay

to cry out against
the killer who cracks the latch.

On the open map, the road
to my house bulges like a vein.

He takes a train, he rents
a car, he lurches in

with an open fly. Sweet Eve
was just the Farmer's Daughter,

he wooed her with a wormy apple.
He's a dirty joke, he's

always everybody's last
lover, he's a regular

can of worms—you wry Medusa,
I am a mongoose staring you down.

SNAKESKIN

Down on the porch, the black
snake sits like a thick fist.
His back is flexed and slick.
The wedge of his forehead turns
to the sun. He does not remember
the skin shucked in the attic,
the high branches of our family tree.

The moth will not recall the flannel
cocoon. The snail empties the endless
convolutions of its shell. Think
of the clear husk of the locust,
sewn like an ear to the elm.
How easily they leave old lives,
as an eager lover steps from the skirts
at her ankles.

           Sleep corrects memory:
the long sleep of bear and woodchuck,
the sleep of the sea,
the sleep of the wooden spool unwinding,
the sleep of snow, when houses lose
their angles and edges, the slow
sleep of no dreaming;

and we could rise up in new skins
to a full confusion of green,
to the slick stalks of grasses,
and the catalpa, that beany tree, offering
its great, white, aromatic promise.

SOUTHERN ARTIFACT

Lue Cinda Prunty Stone, the paper says
you were alive last week at 103,
rocking in a cane-bottom chair,
your breasts in your lap
and your squat legs, solid as bedposts,
wrapped in cotton stockings.
But that was not you.
Long before you sweat in my mother's kitchen,
put up pickles in a crock,
swatted flies with a Sycamore switch,
before you delivered signs and blessings
to black children hunkered down beside you,
before your teeth rotted with snuff,
you had begun to seep away.
All that time you were rocking,
while you turned up to us a stupid, stoic face,
the runners were kneading the red dirt
into a mighty poultice
that slowly sucked you out of yourself,
and you went down into the earth—
willing yourself away without our notice—
until your eyes were only props,
the mouth's singing automatic.
All that was left, Lue Cinda,
when a host of relatives and friends
gathered in Gretna to bury you—
your face, your clothes, the chair, all
that was left was what we had created:
a piece of lore, our mother-lode
of tradition, our nigra mammy.
And if I undid your kerchief
your head would fragment
and the rank pieces of a region
fall quietly into your lap.

AMERICAN AT AUSCHWITZ

I. NEAR CRACOW

Here, by the Vistula:
the stacks of bundled grain
established on the hillside—

how like small men,
heads bowing,
necks bent down by the heavy air,
the pounds of ashes
drifted across the river.
How sympathetic they seem,
morose, guilty. . . .

See.
The mind is fat with suppositions.

II. GUARD'S HOUSE

There is no irony
in the blossoms by the fences,
red geraniums flourishing
by the trellis
where once hung
frail Jewish flowers,
delicate vines
of arms and legs,
ribs like petals,
ready for plucking,
black eyes turning
toward the sun.
Why not accept coincidence—
some modest German gardener
who delighted in
planting, weeding out,
plowing under.

History never repeats.
We must limit our vision.
We must not break and run
when we remember
the victims running,
naked, to their chambers,
their hands covering
their breasts as the nipples darken
the breasts darken
the skin is charred and
turns brown and then
black their hair is singed by
the heat it kinks and
curls it will not lie
still it springs up
on their heads their lips
peel back puff out blow up
their tongues swell in
their mouths their speech thickens
it slows down like molasses
the white guards are laughing
in white gowns they are laughing,
the dogs are showing
their white, ridiculous
teeth, and the late sky ripens
like a bruise.

STORK

There are seventeen species of stork.
The painted stork is pink in his nuptial plumage.
The milky stork woos with his large flat bill.
The marabou offers her carrion, as does the adjutant.
Due to irregular throat structure, storks have no voice;
they strike their beaks together in lovesong.
Newborns know to swallow the fish head-first.
In the myth of the moon-bird, storks impregnate women.
All storks adhere to serial monogamy.
In the mating season, two species are migratory:
the black stork who roosts in platforms in the forests of Poland;
the familiar white stork ("good luck" in Western Europe).
They are surpassed in endurance by none but the arctic tern.
They travel a thousand miles to Africa.
They soar on the thermal current.
They precede the rainy season.
They carry the unborn in from the marshland.
If a stork nests in your chimney, a son will be born.
If a stork nests in your chimney, your house will be empty.
If a stork leaves the nest, that is an omen.
If a stork leaves the nest forever, disaster will strike the area.
If a stork's shadow falls on the rosebush, grief descends to the village.
If a stork is damaged, the weather darkens.
If you kill a stork, kinsmen surround you, clacking long sticks together
      like knives.

SUICIDES

Ink blot, sperm on a slide, a squirm
of minnows from the helicopter's
view, the whales have beached.
All day the volunteers have poked
and prodded, but they will not
turn back. Behind them their salty
element foams and rushes: how often
they sounded the dark layers,
past the lacy skeletons of coral,
the squid preparing his black cloak
for a getaway—the ease of gliding,
motion in the midst of motion,
through water! the pull of water
as they stored breath and dove again
and again, looking for bottom, down
to where fish blossom among the sponges
and fossils, where the plants are meat-
eating and sexual, where the ocean
opens to cold drafts that clamp
an iron vise against the skull.

Graceful in water, they labor now
toward palmetto and tufted
hillocks, the hot sun bleaching
and drying out. Their fins dig into
something solid, the broad flukes
spade, then anchor in the sand.

DIALOGUE: POETICS

for Paul Nelson

1st Voice

Admiring the web, do we
forget the spider? The real
poem is a knife-edge,
quick and clean.

The bird needs
no extra feather, the stone
sits in its own shape.

Consider the weather.

We could say that snow
fills the crotches of the birch
and makes a webbed hand.

We could say,
Look at the graceful line
of falling snow!

The point is: It
falls and falls on trees
and houses, with or
without comment.

ITEM:
Should we record snow
falling on the tamaracks
beside the black Winooski
River, and not the trapper
crouched on the far bank,
who thinks, Such
silence, such order.

ITEM:
Seven stones in a circle make
eight shapes.

ITEM:
Not being birds, we seek our own
windpatterns, fashion
the lute, discover language.

ITEM:
Following the taut strands
that span flower and drainspout,
down the long loops, moving
through the spider's whole house,
we come round to the center
and the patient jewel in its own setting.

SONG

By what wild geese were you spawned
that the birds come up to your hand?
I hear them circle and hover,
afraid to fly down here.
Don't they know how well I sweep
my yard? Hair tied back, I leave
my shoes and go out to listen.
They could come downwind
to my house—jaybirds, snowbirds—wing
their wild dance in and out of pine
trees and twist the gray worms down
their bright tongues.

The seeds are scattered, the suet
hangs in the birch tree. Each night
the tree frogs sing to my window:
       brekkit   *brekkit*

FOR S.,

this girl who is
twisting her lovely face to tell me—
something, her body is
rigid with
language, under her pink blouse
her shoulders
stiffen, her left
hand jerks out a
rhythm to sing by,
the vowels clog in her throat, the
improbable consonants won't
come, she
pauses,
a phrase,
a sentence a whole thought
tumble out on their own,
she tries to catch that tide of language,
then hangs
on one
word, she
labors
for speech,
past inadequate body,
past the rural scene
of the window, past the beasts
busy with lunch, the flowers tied
to the field, each a separate
cup of juices, and the stones
with their mouths sewn shut.

II

FARM WIFE

Dark as the spring river, the earth
opens each damp row as the farmer
swings the far side of the field.
The blackbirds flash their red
wing patches and wheel in his wake,
down to the black dirt; the windmill
grinds in its chain rig and tower.

In the kitchen, his wife is baking.
She stands in the door in her long white
gloves of flour. She cocks her head and
tries to remember, turns like the moon
toward the sea-black field. Her belly
is rising, her apron fills like a sail.
She is gliding now, the windmill churns
beneath her, she passes the farmer,
the fine map of the furrows.
The neighbors point to the bone-white
spot in the sky.

Let her float
like a fat gull that swoops and circles,
before her husband comes in for supper,
before her children grow up and leave her,
before the pulley cranks her down
the dark shaft, and the church blesses
her stone bed, and the earth seals
its black mouth like a scar.

"THE WIFE TAKES A CHILD"

She has come next door to practice our piano.
Fat worms, her fingers hover over the keys,
dolce, dolce, advance to a black note.
I call out answers; she blinks a trusting eye.
From the window I can see the phlox
bank and flower, the violets' broad train
at the yard's edge, and beyond, the bee-boxes,
each one baited for summer with a queen.

Love, how long must we reproduce ourselves
in the neighbors' children, bees in false hives,
bright inviting blossoms, mine for a season.
Against the C-scale's awkward lullabye
I carry the offense of my flat belly,
the silent red loss of monthly bleeding.

THE HANDMAIDEN

Robert Bryant, 1878-1958
Rose Peters Bryant, 1877-1914
Sara Bolling Bryant, 1890-

Five births in eight years, the last
with its terrible flux and no help for it,
their mother was dead, his real wife was dead.
The children parcelled out to relatives,
he fed on his sorrow, that hard red berry—
four years, until duty recalled them
and drove his famous temper underground.

After careful interview, she was installed;
gave little, was given little;
prepared the biscuit; instructed
the children by his strict example;
watched them flutter from the house like kites;
stood by as he reeled them back in
on memory's long string.
                     At his death,
his will supplanted all imagination.
What did it matter, to have survived him?
Daily she ties on her bonnet, walks
the half mile to rake, mow or mulch
his family plot. There the two bodies
nestle together under the common stone:
Robert on the left, her own lot to the right,
and at the center his grief-perfected Rose.

GATHERING

When the folds of the curtain drew apart, you were sitting in the third row with her, she was slim and beautiful, her mouth was a ripe, purple berry, above the elegant nose her eyes were two roaches, she *wasn't* beautiful, her breasts were cones under the black crepe, she had no hips at all, her hair stroked your cheek like a web. I ran from the stage and drove through rain on the five-lane highway. Behind the barricade the van waited like an oven, the doors were folded back and slick with rain. They were bringing in the bodies from the sea each one wrapped in burlap. Long, slender cigars, how easily they slid into that open mouth.

*   *   *

It was a party. It was a reunion of old friends. It was out on the lawn behind a beautiful house. The shrubbery was old and expensive, the house in need of repair. Beside the stone fence, a cast-iron pot held the dinner. Everyone laughed and chatted. The women in sharkskin dresses displayed triangular swatches of tan. I was lying in the living room. I was not allowed in the sun. I was lying on the antique horsehair sofa, in need of repair. Someone said My God she sunburned in the shade. Everyone laughed. Someone said After all she's twelve months pregnant. Everyone laughed. I noticed the hem had come out of my dress. I noticed my bedroom slippers. I noticed my red legs against the expensive sofa. The young Greek came up and took my hand. After all she's twelve months pregnant, he said. No one said a word. The cook, in a clean apron, brought hot water in the pot, which was old and in need of repair. Outside, the ice, like laughter, was lethal against the expensive crystal.

*   *   *

I made no move to stop it, I did nothing but watch, I was standing at the top of the stairs and suddenly my arms were weak, the baby started to roll, away from me, out toward the vertical space above the staggered brown keyboard, she was water, graceful, unhurried, she was moving away from me, down across the elbows, along the limp forearms, the ball bearings of the wrists pushed her forward, over the thumbmound, the headline and heartline, she polished my gold ring with her rolling, heading toward the fingers' offering gesture. But slowly the hand closed like a dried leaf, the palm was curling, the thumb moved up to a pinch, and hooked at last the last end of the small, flowered, flannel nightgown.

BIRTHDAY SESTINA

for Ola Dudley Yeatts

A crowded nursery, your shelf holds eighteen
photographs, grandchildren and their children,
gray and glossy, each forever a baby.
Across the room, facing down your daughters'
bounty: gazing from a gauzy dream
of Renoir yellows, blues and rose: your picture

over the bedstead. You brought the gilt-edged picture
and bone china to your groom's house—eighteen
months in Penhook, Va., you bawled like a baby.
He was the sixth of eight industrious children;
good stock, but not the chevalier you were dreaming
of. Queen of the Piedmont, the spoiled daughter

of your father's house, oh you were beauty's daughter
with a starched waist and high-swept hair! At eighteen,
before he wooed and wed you, could you picture
him by the wagon, you holding the baby?
The growing yield, a wagonload of children?
How he harvested, year on year, his dreamy

seed's worth! Married to routine, you dreamed
of your father, cried out with fever. In 1918
Papa almost lost you and the baby
you carried. The croup kettle steamed your picture
from its frame. My mother, your oldest daughter,
hid in the closet like a shoe. Children

were dying everywhere. You fed your children
whiskey and sugar, embraced the milky dream
of vapor, nursing the flu like another daughter.
But frailty failed you, gave way to health and eighteen
times remembering as the mantel's picture
gallery flourished and fattened, one baby

after another. Mothers now, we baby
you like the last rose, surround you with children.
Composed beneath your pastel, brass-edged picture,
you choose the veil of cataracts. In the dream
he calls with a soft voice, *Daughter, Daughter,*
and you are beautiful, high-minded, and eighteen.

CLAIMING KIN

Insistent as a whistle, her voice up
the stairs pried open the blanket's
tight lid and piped me
down to the pressure cooker's steam and rattle.
In my mother's kitchen, the hot iron spit
on signal, the vacuum cleaner whined
and snuffled. Bright face
and a snazzy apron, clicking her long spoons,
how she commandeered the razzle-dazzle!

In the front room I dabbed
the company chairs with a sullen rag.
Pale lump blinking at the light,
I could hear her sing in her shiny kingdom,
the sound drifted out like a bottled message.
It was the voice of a young girl,
who stopped to gather cool moss,
forgetting the errand, spilling the cornmeal,
and cried and cried in her bearish papa's ear.

At night, while I flopped like a fish
on grandma's spool bed, up from her bed
and my wheezing father she rose to the holly,
flat-leaf and Virginia Creeper.
Soft ghost, plush as a pillow,
she wove and fruited against the black hours:
red berries and running cedar, green signatures
on the table, on the mantel.

Mother, this poem is from your middle
child who, like your private second self
rising at night to wander the dark house,
grew in the shady places:
a green plant in a brass pot,
rootbound, without blossoms.

SISTER

I.

Mother's illness pulled you
home on the first bus, me in your wake.
Day and night you illuminate her room,
sponging distress from that body,
commanding plants into blossom.
Now, between shifts, we sit like friends
in the kitchen, sharing coffee.

In my favorite snapshot you lean
from your tricycle, arms encircling me—
moon-faced, myopic, immobile
in my blue snowsuit—as if by sheer will
you could lift me on. Who can deny
the gravity of that embrace?
Displaced from my life,
once more angling for this family,
I glide into orbit.

Is it your power to hurt them
I am jealous of?

II.

In the recurring dream I am six or seven.
We live in the little house with its yardful of oak,
that treasure of brown hands I raked and piled.
Yes, say my parents, we have the child you need:
they have come for me, two men in suits, carrying machetes.
Outside, under the oaks, the crowd awaits the ceremony.
I've made a perfect likeness—
same pie face, limp hair, same muslin feedsack gown,
like yours, except the ribbon at the neck is blue.
But when they draw the knives and hack off my head,

rags, string, sawdust, everything pours out but blood
and they know, they will not forgive.
Then we are in the car, driving to Danville,
Mother and Daddy are in the back with me.
As we cross the Banister River Bridge I look down;
my hand sweats on the handle:
leap out and fall to that red sash,
or stay in the car, sweeping toward the blade—

III.

O the houses we inhabited—
saplings in a rough square,
a mossy patch, a circle drawn in dirt
and you settled us in.
How to resist the old cookstove,
bright as a tooth in the deep woods?
The nest sat on the rack, a big gray cake,
and when you opened the oven
out of it issued the hornets
with their instinctive venom,
streaming from that stiff breast,
and you went flying down the path,
screaming for Momma, dragging
home your long lethal tail.

*

You midpoint on the stairs, flush with argument;
my father below, rising from his cushion;

you scuttling up and out of reach;
my father settling back with the last word;

visible knees, reproach flung down to the chair,
my father rises with his rolled newspaper,

scuffle of feet, heavy footsteps following—
door slams, locks.

*

You with your tall slender body,
your beaux on the stoop, your local husband,
you with the easy charm you learned from your mother,
you with your talent for children, your perfect loaves,
your sewing machine, that cabinet of bees,
your fierce scissors laboring over cloth and hair
to wreak my transformation.

*

You,
pulling me home in the wagon,
breakneck with your bleating cargo,
until I put out my foot to slow us
and the secret piece of tin
sliced it like a tomato.

*

When we were little
I used to wish you dead;
then hold my breath and sweat
to hear yours
release, intake, relax into sleep.

IV.

We were playing on the grassy hill
on the long side of the house—a clot
of cousins, all of them boys, all older,
a noisy cluster rearranging its cells,
when the upstairs left window split
its voile curtains and my aunt
leaned out into summer to holler
down at us, calling *me*, holding
out of the window like a flag,
like a dead bird, the britches I'd peed in
and hidden under Grandma Sally's bed.
The rest is the story I was raised on:
how I crouched around back, washing
them out, while you sat on a slab
of rock by the spigot and cried.

V.

Anyone else, you would have died. Toxic
in the womb, weighing in early at less
than five pounds, all of it nerve and reckless
appetite, you couldn't even stomach
Mother's milk. Not just the usual colic
and croup for you; brandishing your flair
for the acute, you'd sniff out whatever
disease or disaster was lurking in the district.

Your fourth year was charted like a fever.
With my routine appearance, what could she do
but leave me penned to endlessly reassemble
the coffeepot? As she sponged you by the hour
you thrashed the bed, your eyes swam back in your skull
and you nearly bit your purple tongue in two.

A neighbor called for equipment:
whatever embers from the hearth
lay dormant in the basket I'd
tossed into the shed,
fed on the gas-soaked floor
and the shed caught in the wind,
sprouted a great orange growth
that spread to the left
where the feeder calves were penned,
to the right and the dog lots,
bridged to the fence on sumac
where it ran that plank border
eating creosote, ringing
the yard, the house, all of us
at lunch in the kitchen,
with such symmetry:
        the family
        the circle of fire

THE HEN

The neck lodged under a stick,
the stick under her foot,
she held the full white breast
with both hands, yanked up and out,
and the head was delivered of the body.
Brain stuck like a lens; the profile
fringed with red feathers.
Deposed, abstracted,
the head lay on the ground like a coin.
But the rest, released into the yard,
language and direction wrung from it,
flapped the insufficient wings
and staggered forward, convulsed, instinctive—
I thought it was sobbing to see it hump the dust,
pulsing out those muddy juices,
as if something, deep in the gizzard,
in the sack of soft nuggets,
drove it toward the amputated member.
Even then, watching it litter the ground
with snowy refusals, I knew it was this
that held life, gave life,
and not the head with its hard contemplative eye.

THE FEAST OF THE ASSUMPTION OF THE VIRGIN

Matins

Felix rapina. The flap
and whistle of the angel's
wings, the public birth,
the chastened motherhood.
When they led her from her son's
cruel scaffolding, she wanted
no more miracles. Now this.
Plucked up to heaven, a pressed
flower—her body is used
for a million statuary.

Nones

The church sweats in its dark stone.
The triptych, a pamphlet of roses,
flanks the altar. In one stained
panel of window, Joseph provides detail.
The Madonna mourns from a nearby table;
one hand is raised
as if reaching for fruit. Among
the murmuring candles, a solicitor
spews his secret into her ear.

Mary,
Holy Vessel, Queen of the Martyrs:
in the mountains of Zakopane

the rutted street swells
with women, bringing you flowers.
See how they cradle

the passionate blossoms. Precious
Mother, the village is blooming. Here,
in a row by the plain wood houses,

here, by the roadside,
the young girls are gathered.
Each wears white lace, hand-made

for marriage; each
is chosen, blessed by the father;
and when the bells release

a shower of pollen,
each mouth opens to rapture
like a wound.

III

DAMAGE

It didn't suckle. That
was the first indication.

Looking back, I know how much I knew.
The repetitious bloodfall,

the grating at the door of bone,
the afterbirth stuck in my womb like a scab.

Others were lucky,
response was taken from them.

Each time I bathe him
in his little tub, I think

How easy to let go

Let go

HOUSE

This orphaned house. Its needs, its presences.

Something brought us here—how else
could we, raw mourners,
have found it
tucked under the hill beside the sea?

Everything still stands
from previous lives: well, woodstove,
the feather tick imprinted
with so many bodies.

This place survives their multiple
amputations. The tug on the nipple
after the baby is gone,
after the breast is gone.

Trimming the wicks, setting the oak table—
when I move the air gives,
feels polished, I fill
the waiting sleeve with movement.

And everywhere the proprietary swallows.

    *   *   *

The body learns to incorporate its pain.
Sorrow lodged in the kitchen.
Stepsister. She-who-remembers. There,
in the corner, she worked her practical
arts—intaglio and salt-cure:

> A splash of brine on the table,
> hot iron, knife-slip, a scar,
> a trough, the table webs
> with stains and scratches.

Deep into the water's
grain, a boat engraves
its habits. The wake
has healed but retains
the shape of the hull,
the wound of the rudder.

*   *   *

I have my routine.

The garden calls me to its harvesting.
The well needs me to draw up water.

From the seawind, I read tomorrow's
weather. The swallows surround us.

Evenings, we sit inside,
under the wing of the unfinished attic.

Here, in this place, this parentage,
we live with loss, a child's repeating absence.

THE LETTER

She sits at the table
with her small collection of treasure.
Chooses from it a shell whose delicate edges whorl
inward to a palm, a lifeprint.
Inside this pastel saucer,
parsley and chives recall a Japanese garden:
clean, immutable.
If only she were there,
a single tiny figure by the pool,
holding the letter.
If only she were rock, tree, clear water.

APRIL, 1945

Soft *chink*—
a dog stretching its chain in sleep,
but he has no dog. Beside him,
his wife's nasal exhalation.
Cinched his pyjamas. Plucked
the gun, erect, from the corner.
Stalked the dark house, along
the striped oak toward linoleum.
Sprawling there, saw her nightgown
filling the bedroom doorway as if
on the washline, bright with sun,
supple, inhaling, gathering light
and wind to its center, its bosom,
that wet red sponge.

THE WANING MOON

Couched in pillows, coaching him
toward her open blouse and its ripe
nipple, feeling the bite, the shudder,
thinking

This is mine

she always wanted children—boys
with soft purses between their legs,
girls to call help or Mama, the purple
bundle to crack from her thighs,
a lump inside her

Here is the skull
here the foot split from a fin

And before, her body grown useful,
the salty waters gathering. And loss:
month after month, the seed
is hosed from its hammock.

At night, she sifts the dried
dillweed, worries the bread dough
into a long loaf. And when her husband
rolls toward her in the brass bed,
she chooses chastity.

EXECUTIONER

You were a man with only your own resources,
nothing to stand on, no rope, no rafters.
Alone in your cell,
you tied your belt to the grill
of the window and leaned into death,
such labor that never relinquished
until your lungs folded like tissue,
until your temples were brought to blossom
and the heart, in its conviction, overcome.

THE VICTIM

Who could remember cause? Both
sought injury, and God knows
they were perfectly matched for pain.
Fenced into their landscape of passion,
each moved to the center and set upon
the other. Always, she would deploy
the tease, the jab, the deft tongue,
until his arm swung out on its hinge,
coming flat-handed against her face,
recoiled, then stiffened to thrust
his fist into her open mouth.
This was not the only violation.
When a child is struck by her father,
she crawls toward him, not away,
bound by habits not yet broken.

THE BURIAL

Vermont, 1889

March, when the ground softened
and the men could dig the multiple graves,
was time enough to examine the winter's losses.
But the girl from Lower Cabot—
when they opened the coffins
to match the dead to their markers,
they found the corpse in terrific disarray:
bodice torn from the throat,
face sealed in distortion, eyes
open, the coins nowhere in evidence,
and in each fist a wad of her own dark hair.

THE MARRIAGE

Under its angry skin, her grief
ripens: succulent, wound-color.
She knew there were other women—
his baroque excuses for silence—
but knew in the weaker hemisphere
of her heart, that stringent
muscle pumping in, valved open.
Hinged clam, living for fifteen years
on grit and gravel, housed now against
the weather, she has the car, the kids,
an appetite for garbage. He's got
a new wife, wants her to take him in,
produce a pearl.

THE BIRTH

The first would be five now.
She remembers herself in family photos,
dark hair braided and bandaged.
She had to work
at the second, Scorpio,
who skulks through her dreams
distempered and bony. But this one—
full-term, sharp-chinned, surfacing
face up—needs no such conjuring. She says,
"This is your son," fingering
the rosary of his spine. You scan
her pouchy belly. You study the phonebook.
You pocket your great thumbs.
You step off the distance of the room.
Applying the active mouth like a leech,
she feels the persuasive bloodbeat,
unfurls the fist, the palm
already mapped and pencilled in.

THE DROWNED MAN

How I love you in your hopeless act.
The black wound on the skin of the pond;
the small body already stiffening:
and so you entered that dark closet of water.

But your wife on the shore
turned away from the lost child,
chose the two live children rooted behind her
receiving the permanent visions of their sleep,
chose life,
chose to live with ice at the heart.

HARVEST

The farmer circles the pasture
checking fences. Deep
in the broomstraw, the dove withholds

her three notes. The sky
to the southwest is uniformly
blue. Years of plowing under

have brought this red clay to its
green conclusion.
Down back,

the herd
clusters to the loading pen.
Only disease or dogpack

could alter such order. Is that
what he asks for in the late
fields, the falling afternoon?

THE QUICKENING

All evening she shifts through the house,
gathering purpose.
Everything is changed now,
she has money in her purse,
she has a weapon.
The moon, snagged in the oak,
is rising out of its black hand,
lights the bedroom.
Under that grim eye,
the bed is luminous, refractive.
As he steps incautiously into its white field,
she will be waiting, approximating sleep:
Like the baby suspended inside her.
Like a hawk adrift in its fine solution of clouds.

THE VISIT

The afternoon spreads its fingers on the lawn,
and such light as penetrates the shrubs
enters the house with hesitation.
I have come from a great distance
to find my father asleep in his large brown chair.
Why isn't he out in the fields, our common passion?
I want to wake him with kisses,
I want to reach out and stroke his hand.
But I turn away, without speech or gesture,
having for so long withheld my body from him.

ALL SOULS' DAY

Confronting frost,
the trees assume their attitudes of pain.
Who can think of the ocean?
its permanent surf, its violated sand.

She takes off her glasses,
folds them into their tapestry
envelope. After coffee,
after she straightens the kitchen,
after her TV program,
she is going to pray for the children.

Scarved and suited for autumn,
she will stand, as in the park,
where they are gathered, that each
may sail his little sin into temperate waters.